50 Greek Yogurt Recipes for Home

By: Kelly Johnson

Table of Contents

- Greek Yogurt Parfait with Fresh Berries
- Honey Greek Yogurt Dip for Fruit
- Greek Yogurt Pancakes
- Tzatziki Sauce
- Greek Yogurt and Berry Smoothie
- Greek Yogurt Chicken Salad
- Greek Yogurt and Cucumber Salad
- Lemon Blueberry Greek Yogurt Muffins
- Greek Yogurt Chicken Souvlaki
- Greek Yogurt Caesar Salad Dressing
- Greek Yogurt Spinach Artichoke Dip
- Greek Yogurt Ranch Dressing
- Greek Yogurt and Granola Breakfast Bowl
- Greek Yogurt Chocolate Chip Cookies
- Greek Yogurt and Dill Potato Salad
- Greek Yogurt Cheesecake
- Greek Yogurt Coleslaw
- Greek Yogurt Pesto Pasta
- Greek Yogurt and Herb Grilled Chicken
- Greek Yogurt Fruit Salad
- Greek Yogurt and Avocado Dip
- Greek Yogurt Tandoori Chicken Skewers
- Greek Yogurt Caesar Salad
- Greek Yogurt Chicken Gyros
- Greek Yogurt Ranch Chicken Wings
- Greek Yogurt and Berry Popsicles
- Greek Yogurt Veggie Dip
- Greek Yogurt Chicken Curry
- Greek Yogurt and Herb Quinoa Salad
- Greek Yogurt Lemon Bars
- Greek Yogurt Chicken Tzatziki Wrap
- Greek Yogurt Hummus
- Greek Yogurt Raspberry Tart
- Greek Yogurt and Cucumber Gazpacho
- Greek Yogurt and Herb Stuffed Mushrooms

- Greek Yogurt and Honey Mustard Chicken
- Greek Yogurt and Lemon Herb Salmon
- Greek Yogurt and Berry Breakfast Pizza
- Greek Yogurt and Cilantro Lime Rice
- Greek Yogurt Berry Popsicles
- Greek Yogurt Chicken Fajitas
- Greek Yogurt Avocado Toast
- Greek Yogurt and Herb Zucchini Noodles
- Greek Yogurt Tiramisu
- Greek Yogurt and Honey Glazed Carrots
- Greek Yogurt Chicken Caesar Wrap
- Greek Yogurt and Pumpkin Bread
- Greek Yogurt and Berry Cobbler
- Greek Yogurt and Herb Stuffed Chicken Breast
- Greek Yogurt and Chia Seed Pudding

Greek Yogurt Parfait with Fresh Berries

Ingredients:

- 1 cup Greek yogurt (full-fat or low-fat)
- 1 tablespoon honey or maple syrup
- 1 teaspoon vanilla extract
- 1 cup mixed fresh berries (strawberries, blueberries, raspberries)
- 1/4 cup granola
- 2 tablespoons chopped nuts (almonds, walnuts, or pistachios)
- Fresh mint leaves for garnish (optional)

Instructions:

Prepare Greek Yogurt Mixture:
- In a bowl, combine Greek yogurt, honey (or maple syrup), and vanilla extract. Mix well until smooth.

Assemble Parfait:
- In serving glasses or bowls, start by layering a spoonful of the Greek yogurt mixture at the bottom.

Add Fresh Berries:
- Add a layer of mixed fresh berries on top of the Greek yogurt.

Repeat Layers:
- Repeat the layers until you reach the top of the glass or bowl, finishing with a dollop of Greek yogurt on the top.

Top with Granola and Nuts:
- Sprinkle granola evenly over the top layer of Greek yogurt.
- Add a generous sprinkle of chopped nuts.

Garnish:
- Garnish with fresh mint leaves for a burst of freshness (optional).

Serve:
- Serve the Greek Yogurt Parfait immediately as a delightful and healthy breakfast or snack.

Enjoy:
- Grab a spoon and enjoy the creamy Greek yogurt, sweet berries, crunchy granola, and nutty goodness in every bite!

Feel free to customize this parfait by adding your favorite fruits, swapping out the nuts, or incorporating other toppings like coconut flakes or a drizzle of additional honey. It's a versatile and delicious treat that's as pleasing to the eyes as it is to the taste buds.

Honey Greek Yogurt Dip for Fruit

Ingredients:

- 1 cup Greek yogurt
- 2 tablespoons honey (adjust to taste)
- 1 teaspoon vanilla extract
- Zest of 1 lemon (optional)
- Assorted fresh fruits for dipping (strawberries, apple slices, grapes, pineapple chunks)

Instructions:

Prepare the Greek Yogurt Base:
- In a bowl, combine Greek yogurt, honey, and vanilla extract.

Mix Thoroughly:
- Mix the ingredients thoroughly until the honey is well incorporated into the Greek yogurt.

Add Lemon Zest (Optional):
- If desired, add the zest of one lemon to enhance the freshness of the dip. Mix well.

Chill (Optional):
- For a slightly firmer consistency, you can chill the dip in the refrigerator for 30 minutes before serving.

Serve:
- Transfer the Honey Greek Yogurt Dip to a serving bowl.

Prepare Fruit for Dipping:
- Wash and prepare a variety of fresh fruits for dipping. This can include strawberries, apple slices, grapes, and pineapple chunks.

Serve and Enjoy:
- Arrange the prepared fruit around the bowl of Honey Greek Yogurt Dip.
- Serve immediately and enjoy this delightful and wholesome fruit dip!

Feel free to adjust the sweetness by adding more or less honey according to your taste preference. This versatile dip is not only delicious but also a healthy way to enjoy your favorite fruits.

Greek Yogurt Pancakes

Ingredients:

- 1 cup all-purpose flour
- 1 tablespoon sugar
- 1 teaspoon baking powder
- 1/2 teaspoon baking soda
- 1/4 teaspoon salt
- 1 cup Greek yogurt
- 1/2 cup milk
- 2 large eggs
- 1 teaspoon vanilla extract
- Butter or oil for cooking
- Maple syrup and fresh berries for serving

Instructions:

Prepare Dry Ingredients:
- In a large mixing bowl, whisk together the flour, sugar, baking powder, baking soda, and salt.

Prepare Wet Ingredients:
- In another bowl, combine Greek yogurt, milk, eggs, and vanilla extract. Mix until well combined.

Combine Wet and Dry Ingredients:
- Pour the wet ingredients into the dry ingredients. Stir until just combined. Do not overmix; it's okay if there are a few lumps.

Let the Batter Rest:
- Allow the batter to rest for 5-10 minutes. This helps the ingredients meld and results in fluffier pancakes.

Heat the Griddle or Pan:
- Preheat a griddle or non-stick pan over medium heat. Add a small amount of butter or oil to coat the surface.

Cook the Pancakes:
- Pour 1/4 cup portions of batter onto the griddle for each pancake. Cook until bubbles form on the surface, and the edges begin to set, about 2-3 minutes.

Flip and Cook:

- Flip the pancakes and cook for an additional 1-2 minutes on the other side, or until golden brown.

Repeat:
- Repeat until all the batter is used, adding more butter or oil to the griddle as needed.

Serve:
- Serve the Greek Yogurt Pancakes warm, topped with maple syrup and fresh berries.

Enjoy:
- Enjoy these light and fluffy pancakes with the added richness and protein from Greek yogurt!

Feel free to customize these pancakes by adding ingredients like blueberries, chocolate chips, or chopped nuts to the batter before cooking. These pancakes are a delicious and nutritious breakfast option.

Tzatziki Sauce

Ingredients:

- 1 cup Greek yogurt
- 1 cucumber, finely grated and drained
- 2 cloves garlic, minced
- 1 tablespoon fresh dill, chopped
- 1 tablespoon fresh mint, chopped (optional)
- 1 tablespoon extra virgin olive oil
- 1 teaspoon lemon juice
- Salt and pepper to taste

Instructions:

Prepare the Cucumber:
- Finely grate the cucumber using a box grater. Place the grated cucumber in a fine mesh sieve or cheesecloth, and squeeze out excess liquid.

Combine Ingredients:
- In a bowl, combine the Greek yogurt, grated and drained cucumber, minced garlic, chopped dill, chopped mint (if using), extra virgin olive oil, and lemon juice.

Mix Well:
- Mix all the ingredients until well combined.

Season:
- Season the tzatziki sauce with salt and pepper to taste. Adjust the seasoning according to your preference.

Chill (Optional):
- For enhanced flavors, refrigerate the tzatziki sauce for at least 30 minutes before serving.

Serve:
- Transfer the tzatziki sauce to a serving bowl.

Garnish (Optional):
- Garnish with a drizzle of olive oil and a sprig of fresh dill or mint if desired.

Enjoy:
- Serve the tzatziki sauce as a refreshing dip with pita bread, as a sauce for grilled meats, or as a condiment for gyros. Enjoy the cool and tangy flavors!

Feel free to adjust the consistency of the tzatziki by adding more or less cucumber, depending on how thick or thin you prefer the sauce. This versatile sauce adds a burst of freshness to a variety of dishes.

Greek Yogurt and Berry Smoothie

Ingredients:

- 1 cup Greek yogurt (plain or vanilla-flavored)
- 1 cup mixed berries (strawberries, blueberries, raspberries)
- 1 ripe banana
- 1/2 cup almond milk or any milk of your choice
- 1 tablespoon honey or maple syrup (optional, depending on sweetness preference)
- Ice cubes (optional)

Instructions:

Prepare the Ingredients:
- Wash the berries and peel the ripe banana.

Combine in Blender:
- In a blender, add Greek yogurt, mixed berries, peeled banana, almond milk, and honey or maple syrup if using.

Blend Until Smooth:
- Blend the ingredients until smooth and creamy. If the consistency is too thick, you can add more almond milk to reach your desired thickness.

Taste and Adjust:
- Taste the smoothie and adjust sweetness by adding more honey or maple syrup if needed.

Add Ice Cubes (Optional):
- If you prefer a colder and icier smoothie, you can add a handful of ice cubes to the blender and blend until well incorporated.

Blend Again (Optional):
- Blend once more if you added ice cubes until the smoothie reaches a slushy consistency.

Serve:
- Pour the Greek Yogurt and Berry Smoothie into glasses.

Garnish (Optional):
- Garnish with additional berries on top for a decorative touch.

Enjoy:
- Enjoy this refreshing and nutritious Greek Yogurt and Berry Smoothie immediately as a quick and healthy breakfast or snack!

Feel free to customize this smoothie by adding other fruits, such as mango or pineapple, or incorporating a handful of spinach for a green boost. It's a versatile and delicious way to enjoy the goodness of Greek yogurt and the vibrant flavors of berries.

Greek Yogurt Chicken Salad

Ingredients:

For the Chicken:

- 1 lb (about 450g) boneless, skinless chicken breasts
- 1 tablespoon olive oil
- 1 teaspoon dried oregano
- 1 teaspoon garlic powder
- Salt and pepper to taste

For the Salad:

- 1 cup Greek yogurt
- 1 cucumber, diced
- 1 cup cherry tomatoes, halved
- 1/2 red onion, finely chopped
- 1/4 cup Kalamata olives, pitted and sliced
- 1/4 cup feta cheese, crumbled
- Fresh parsley, chopped, for garnish

For the Dressing:

- 2 tablespoons extra virgin olive oil
- 1 tablespoon red wine vinegar
- 1 teaspoon Dijon mustard
- Salt and pepper to taste

Instructions:

Prepare the Chicken:
- In a bowl, mix olive oil, dried oregano, garlic powder, salt, and pepper. Coat the chicken breasts with this mixture.
- Heat a grill pan or skillet over medium-high heat. Grill the chicken for 6-8 minutes per side or until fully cooked. Allow it to rest before slicing.

Make the Dressing:

- In a small bowl, whisk together extra virgin olive oil, red wine vinegar, Dijon mustard, salt, and pepper. Set aside.

Prepare the Salad:
- In a large bowl, combine Greek yogurt, diced cucumber, cherry tomatoes, red onion, Kalamata olives, and crumbled feta cheese.

Slice the Chicken:
- Slice the grilled chicken breasts into thin strips.

Assemble the Salad:
- Add the sliced chicken to the bowl with the salad ingredients.

Add Dressing:
- Pour the prepared dressing over the salad and toss everything together until well coated.

Garnish:
- Garnish the Greek Yogurt Chicken Salad with fresh parsley.

Serve:
- Serve immediately and enjoy this light and flavorful chicken salad with the creamy goodness of Greek yogurt.

This Greek Yogurt Chicken Salad is perfect for a wholesome lunch or dinner. It combines the lean protein of grilled chicken with the freshness of vegetables and the richness of Greek yogurt. Feel free to customize with your favorite Greek salad ingredients.

Greek Yogurt and Cucumber Salad

Ingredients:

- 2 cups Greek yogurt (full-fat or low-fat)
- 2 large cucumbers, peeled and diced
- 1/2 red onion, finely chopped
- 2 cloves garlic, minced
- 1/4 cup fresh dill, chopped
- 2 tablespoons extra virgin olive oil
- 1 tablespoon red wine vinegar
- Salt and pepper to taste

Instructions:

Prepare the Ingredients:
- Peel and dice the cucumbers.
- Finely chop the red onion.
- Mince the garlic.
- Chop the fresh dill.

Combine Greek Yogurt and Vegetables:
- In a large bowl, combine Greek yogurt, diced cucumbers, chopped red onion, minced garlic, and chopped fresh dill.

Make the Dressing:
- In a small bowl, whisk together extra virgin olive oil, red wine vinegar, salt, and pepper.

Add Dressing to Salad:
- Pour the dressing over the Greek yogurt and vegetable mixture.

Toss and Chill:
- Gently toss everything together until well combined.
- Refrigerate the salad for at least 30 minutes before serving to allow the flavors to meld.

Adjust Seasoning:
- Before serving, taste and adjust the salt and pepper according to your preference.

Serve:
- Serve the Greek Yogurt and Cucumber Salad chilled.

Garnish (Optional):

- Garnish with additional dill or a drizzle of olive oil if desired.

Enjoy:
- Enjoy this refreshing and creamy Greek Yogurt and Cucumber Salad as a side dish or a light snack.

Feel free to customize this salad by adding cherry tomatoes, olives, or crumbled feta cheese for additional flavors. It's a simple and healthy dish that complements a variety of meals.

Lemon Blueberry Greek Yogurt Muffins

Ingredients:

- 2 cups all-purpose flour
- 1/2 cup granulated sugar
- 1 teaspoon baking powder
- 1/2 teaspoon baking soda
- 1/4 teaspoon salt
- 1 cup Greek yogurt (plain or vanilla)
- 1/4 cup unsalted butter, melted
- 2 large eggs
- 1 teaspoon vanilla extract
- Zest of 1 lemon
- 1 tablespoon lemon juice
- 1 1/2 cups fresh blueberries

Instructions:

Preheat the Oven:
- Preheat your oven to 375°F (190°C). Line a muffin tin with paper liners or grease it lightly.

Prepare Dry Ingredients:
- In a large bowl, whisk together the flour, sugar, baking powder, baking soda, and salt.

Prepare Wet Ingredients:
- In another bowl, mix together the Greek yogurt, melted butter, eggs, vanilla extract, lemon zest, and lemon juice until well combined.

Combine Wet and Dry Ingredients:
- Add the wet ingredients to the dry ingredients and gently fold until just combined. Be careful not to overmix.

Fold in Blueberries:
- Gently fold in the fresh blueberries until evenly distributed throughout the batter.

Fill Muffin Cups:
- Spoon the batter into the muffin cups, filling each about 2/3 full.

Bake:
- Bake in the preheated oven for 18-20 minutes or until a toothpick inserted into the center comes out clean.

Cool:
- Allow the muffins to cool in the tin for 5 minutes, then transfer them to a wire rack to cool completely.

Optional Glaze (Optional):
- If desired, you can drizzle the cooled muffins with a simple glaze made with powdered sugar and lemon juice.

Serve and Enjoy:
- Serve these Lemon Blueberry Greek Yogurt Muffins as a delightful breakfast or snack option.

Feel free to adjust the sweetness by adding more or less sugar according to your preference. The combination of tangy Greek yogurt, bright lemon, and juicy blueberries makes these muffins a delicious and moist treat.

Greek Yogurt Chicken Souvlaki

Ingredients:

For the Marinade:

- 1.5 lbs (about 700g) boneless, skinless chicken breasts, cut into bite-sized pieces
- 1 cup Greek yogurt
- 3 tablespoons olive oil
- 3 cloves garlic, minced
- 1 tablespoon dried oregano
- 1 teaspoon ground cumin
- 1 teaspoon paprika
- Zest and juice of 1 lemon
- Salt and pepper to taste

For Serving:

- Pita bread or flatbreads
- Tzatziki sauce
- Sliced tomatoes
- Sliced cucumbers
- Red onion, thinly sliced
- Fresh parsley, chopped

Instructions:

Prepare the Marinade:
- In a bowl, combine Greek yogurt, olive oil, minced garlic, dried oregano, ground cumin, paprika, lemon zest, and lemon juice. Mix well.

Season Chicken:
- Season the chicken pieces with salt and pepper.

Marinate Chicken:
- Add the chicken pieces to the marinade, making sure they are well-coated. Cover and refrigerate for at least 2 hours, or preferably overnight for the flavors to develop.

Skewer the Chicken:

- Preheat a grill or grill pan over medium-high heat.
- Thread the marinated chicken pieces onto skewers.

Grill Chicken:
- Grill the chicken skewers for about 6-8 minutes per side or until fully cooked and slightly charred.

Warm Pita Bread:
- While the chicken is grilling, warm the pita bread or flatbreads on the grill or in the oven.

Assemble Souvlaki:
- Once the chicken is cooked, remove it from the skewers.
- Assemble the souvlaki by placing the grilled chicken on warm pita bread or flatbreads.

Add Toppings:
- Top with sliced tomatoes, cucumbers, red onion, and a generous dollop of tzatziki sauce.

Garnish:
- Garnish with chopped fresh parsley.

Serve:
- Serve the Greek Yogurt Chicken Souvlaki immediately.

Enjoy this delicious and flavorful Greek Yogurt Chicken Souvlaki for a taste of Greece right at home. It's a perfect dish for a casual dinner or a summer barbecue.

Greek Yogurt Caesar Salad Dressing

Ingredients:

- 1 cup Greek yogurt (full-fat or low-fat)
- 1/4 cup grated Parmesan cheese
- 2 tablespoons olive oil
- 2 tablespoons lemon juice
- 1 tablespoon Dijon mustard
- 2 cloves garlic, minced
- 1 teaspoon Worcestershire sauce
- Salt and black pepper to taste
- Anchovies (optional), finely minced or anchovy paste

Instructions:

Combine Ingredients:
- In a bowl, combine Greek yogurt, grated Parmesan cheese, olive oil, lemon juice, Dijon mustard, minced garlic, Worcestershire sauce, and anchovies if using.

Whisk Until Smooth:
- Whisk the ingredients together until the dressing is smooth and well combined.

Adjust Consistency:
- If the dressing is too thick, you can thin it out by adding a little water or more lemon juice until you reach your desired consistency.

Season:
- Season the dressing with salt and black pepper to taste. Keep in mind that Parmesan and anchovies can be salty, so adjust accordingly.

Refrigerate (Optional):
- For enhanced flavor, refrigerate the dressing for at least 30 minutes before serving.

Serve:
- Drizzle the Greek Yogurt Caesar Salad Dressing over your favorite Caesar salad ingredients, such as romaine lettuce, croutons, and additional Parmesan cheese.

Toss and Enjoy:
- Toss the salad until the dressing evenly coats the ingredients.

Garnish (Optional):

- Garnish with extra Parmesan shavings and a sprinkle of black pepper if desired.

Serve and Enjoy:
- Serve immediately and enjoy a lighter and healthier Caesar salad with the creamy goodness of Greek yogurt.

This Greek Yogurt Caesar Salad Dressing offers a tangy and creamy twist to the classic dressing. It's a delicious option for those looking for a lighter alternative without sacrificing flavor.

Greek Yogurt Spinach Artichoke Dip

Ingredients:

- 1 cup Greek yogurt (full-fat or low-fat)
- 1 cup frozen chopped spinach, thawed and well-drained
- 1 cup canned artichoke hearts, chopped
- 1 cup shredded mozzarella cheese
- 1/2 cup grated Parmesan cheese
- 1/2 cup mayonnaise
- 2 cloves garlic, minced
- 1 teaspoon onion powder
- 1 teaspoon dried oregano
- 1/2 teaspoon salt
- 1/4 teaspoon black pepper
- Pinch of red pepper flakes (optional)
- Olive oil (for greasing the baking dish)
- Fresh parsley, chopped (for garnish)

Instructions:

Preheat the Oven:
- Preheat your oven to 375°F (190°C).

Grease Baking Dish:
- Grease a baking dish with olive oil.

Mix Ingredients:
- In a large bowl, combine Greek yogurt, chopped spinach, chopped artichoke hearts, mozzarella cheese, Parmesan cheese, mayonnaise, minced garlic, onion powder, dried oregano, salt, black pepper, and red pepper flakes if using. Mix well until all ingredients are evenly combined.

Transfer to Baking Dish:
- Transfer the mixture to the greased baking dish, spreading it out evenly.

Bake:
- Bake in the preheated oven for 25-30 minutes or until the dip is hot and bubbly, and the top is golden brown.

Garnish:
- Remove from the oven and garnish with chopped fresh parsley.

Serve:

- Allow the dip to cool for a few minutes before serving.

Serve and Enjoy:

- Serve this creamy Greek Yogurt Spinach Artichoke Dip with tortilla chips, pita bread, or vegetable sticks.

Feel free to customize this dip by adding a squeeze of lemon juice or adjusting the seasonings to suit your taste. It's a healthier take on the classic spinach artichoke dip without sacrificing any of the delicious flavors.

Greek Yogurt Ranch Dressing

Ingredients:

- 1 cup Greek yogurt (full-fat or low-fat)
- 1/4 cup mayonnaise
- 2 tablespoons fresh chives, chopped
- 2 tablespoons fresh parsley, chopped
- 1 clove garlic, minced
- 1 tablespoon onion powder
- 1 teaspoon dried dill
- 1 teaspoon dried oregano
- 1 teaspoon lemon juice
- Salt and black pepper to taste
- Water (optional, for thinning)

Instructions:

Combine Greek Yogurt and Mayonnaise:
- In a bowl, combine Greek yogurt and mayonnaise. Mix well until smooth.

Add Herbs and Spices:
- Add chopped chives, chopped parsley, minced garlic, onion powder, dried dill, and dried oregano to the yogurt mixture.

Add Lemon Juice:
- Squeeze in fresh lemon juice for a citrusy kick.

Season:
- Season with salt and black pepper to taste. Adjust the quantities according to your preference.

Mix Thoroughly:
- Mix all the ingredients thoroughly until the herbs and spices are evenly distributed.

Check Consistency:
- If you prefer a thinner dressing, you can add a little water, a tablespoon at a time, until you reach your desired consistency.

Refrigerate:
- For the best flavor, refrigerate the dressing for at least 30 minutes before serving to allow the flavors to meld.

Serve:

- Serve the Greek Yogurt Ranch Dressing with salads, vegetables, or as a dip for snacks.

Enjoy:
- Enjoy the creamy and tangy goodness of this healthier version of ranch dressing.

Feel free to customize the dressing by adjusting the herbs and spices to suit your taste.

This Greek Yogurt Ranch Dressing is a lighter alternative to traditional ranch dressing while maintaining the classic flavor.

Greek Yogurt and Granola Breakfast Bowl

Ingredients:

- 1 cup Greek yogurt (full-fat or low-fat)
- 1/2 cup granola (homemade or store-bought)
- 1/2 cup mixed fresh berries (strawberries, blueberries, raspberries)
- 1 tablespoon honey or maple syrup (optional, for drizzling)
- 1 tablespoon nuts or seeds (almonds, walnuts, chia seeds)
- 1 tablespoon shredded coconut (optional)
- Fresh mint leaves for garnish (optional)

Instructions:

Prepare Greek Yogurt Base:
- Spoon the Greek yogurt into a bowl or a serving dish.

Add Granola:
- Sprinkle the granola evenly over the Greek yogurt. This adds a delightful crunch and additional flavor.

Top with Fresh Berries:
- Arrange the mixed fresh berries on top of the granola and yogurt. Be creative with the arrangement for an appealing presentation.

Drizzle with Honey (Optional):
- If you desire added sweetness, drizzle honey or maple syrup over the berries.

Sprinkle Nuts or Seeds:
- Sprinkle nuts or seeds (such as almonds, walnuts, or chia seeds) for extra texture and nutritional benefits.

Optional Coconut Topping:
- If you like coconut, sprinkle shredded coconut over the bowl.

Garnish with Mint (Optional):
- Garnish the breakfast bowl with fresh mint leaves for a burst of freshness.

Serve Immediately:
- Serve the Greek Yogurt and Granola Breakfast Bowl immediately.

Mix Before Eating:
- Before digging in, mix all the ingredients together to combine the creamy yogurt, crunchy granola, and juicy berries.

Enjoy:

- Enjoy this nutritious and delicious breakfast bowl that offers a perfect balance of textures and flavors.

Feel free to customize this breakfast bowl with your favorite toppings, such as sliced bananas, kiwi, or a dollop of nut butter. It's a versatile and satisfying way to start your day on a healthy note.

Greek Yogurt Chocolate Chip Cookies

Ingredients:

- 1 cup all-purpose flour
- 1/2 teaspoon baking soda
- 1/4 teaspoon salt
- 1/4 cup unsalted butter, softened
- 1/2 cup Greek yogurt (plain or vanilla)
- 1/2 cup granulated sugar
- 1/2 cup brown sugar, packed
- 1 large egg
- 1 teaspoon vanilla extract
- 1 cup chocolate chips

Instructions:

Preheat the Oven:
- Preheat your oven to 350°F (175°C). Line a baking sheet with parchment paper.

Combine Dry Ingredients:
- In a bowl, whisk together the flour, baking soda, and salt. Set aside.

Cream Butter and Sugars:
- In a large mixing bowl, cream together the softened butter, granulated sugar, and brown sugar until light and fluffy.

Add Greek Yogurt:
- Add the Greek yogurt to the creamed mixture and mix until well combined.

Add Egg and Vanilla:
- Beat in the egg and vanilla extract until the mixture is smooth.

Incorporate Dry Ingredients:
- Gradually add the dry ingredients to the wet ingredients, mixing just until combined. Be careful not to overmix.

Fold in Chocolate Chips:
- Gently fold in the chocolate chips until evenly distributed throughout the cookie dough.

Scoop Dough onto Baking Sheet:
- Using a cookie scoop or tablespoon, drop rounded portions of dough onto the prepared baking sheet, leaving enough space between each cookie.

Bake:
- Bake in the preheated oven for 10-12 minutes or until the edges are golden brown.

Cool:
- Allow the cookies to cool on the baking sheet for a few minutes before transferring them to a wire rack to cool completely.

Store:
- Store the Greek Yogurt Chocolate Chip Cookies in an airtight container once completely cooled.

Enjoy:
- Enjoy these delicious and slightly healthier chocolate chip cookies with the added goodness of Greek yogurt!

Feel free to experiment with the cookie dough by adding chopped nuts, oats, or different types of chocolate chips. These cookies are a delightful treat that combines the classic flavor of chocolate chip cookies with the creaminess of Greek yogurt.

Greek Yogurt and Dill Potato Salad

Ingredients:

- 2 lbs (about 1 kg) baby potatoes, halved or quartered
- 1 cup Greek yogurt (full-fat or low-fat)
- 3 tablespoons mayonnaise
- 2 tablespoons Dijon mustard
- 1/4 cup fresh dill, chopped
- 1/2 cup red onion, finely chopped
- 2 celery stalks, finely chopped
- 1 tablespoon white wine vinegar
- Salt and black pepper to taste
- Optional: 1/2 cup crumbled feta cheese
- Optional: 1/2 cup sliced Kalamata olives

Instructions:

Boil Potatoes:
- Place the baby potatoes in a large pot of salted water. Bring to a boil and cook until the potatoes are fork-tender. Drain and let them cool.

Make Dressing:
- In a bowl, whisk together Greek yogurt, mayonnaise, Dijon mustard, fresh dill, red onion, celery, white wine vinegar, salt, and black pepper. Mix until well combined.

Assemble Salad:
- Once the potatoes are cooled, gently fold them into the Greek yogurt dressing, ensuring each potato is coated.

Optional Additions:
- If desired, add crumbled feta cheese and sliced Kalamata olives for extra flavor.

Chill:
- Refrigerate the potato salad for at least 1-2 hours to allow the flavors to meld.

Adjust Seasoning:
- Before serving, taste and adjust the seasoning if necessary. Add more salt, pepper, or vinegar according to your preference.

Garnish (Optional):

- Garnish with additional chopped dill before serving.

Serve:
- Serve the Greek Yogurt and Dill Potato Salad as a refreshing side dish for picnics, barbecues, or any meal.

This creamy and tangy potato salad is a healthier alternative to traditional mayonnaise-based recipes, thanks to the Greek yogurt. The addition of dill and optional feta and olives gives it a Mediterranean twist.

Greek Yogurt Cheesecake

Ingredients:

For the Crust:

- 1 1/2 cups graham cracker crumbs
- 1/4 cup unsalted butter, melted
- 1 tablespoon granulated sugar

For the Cheesecake Filling:

- 3 cups Greek yogurt (full-fat or low-fat)
- 3/4 cup granulated sugar
- 3 large eggs
- 1 teaspoon vanilla extract
- 1/4 cup all-purpose flour
- Zest of 1 lemon

For the Topping (Optional):

- Fresh berries or fruit compote

Instructions:

Preheat the Oven:
- Preheat your oven to 325°F (163°C). Grease a 9-inch springform pan.

Prepare the Crust:
- In a bowl, combine graham cracker crumbs, melted butter, and granulated sugar. Press the mixture into the bottom of the prepared springform pan to create an even crust.

Bake the Crust:
- Bake the crust in the preheated oven for 10 minutes. Remove from the oven and let it cool while preparing the filling.

Make the Cheesecake Filling:
- In a large mixing bowl, beat the Greek yogurt, granulated sugar, eggs, vanilla extract, flour, and lemon zest until smooth and well combined.

Pour Filling Over Crust:
- Pour the cheesecake filling over the cooled crust in the springform pan.

Bake the Cheesecake:
- Bake in the preheated oven for 45-50 minutes or until the center is set and the edges are lightly golden.

Cool and Refrigerate:
- Allow the cheesecake to cool in the pan, then refrigerate for at least 4 hours or overnight to set.

Release from Pan:
- Once chilled and set, run a knife around the edges of the pan and release the sides of the springform.

Top with Berries (Optional):
- If desired, top the Greek Yogurt Cheesecake with fresh berries or a fruit compote before serving.

Slice and Serve:
- Slice the cheesecake into wedges and serve chilled.

This Greek Yogurt Cheesecake offers a lighter and tangier twist on the classic dessert.

The Greek yogurt adds a creamy texture and a delightful tanginess, making it a refreshing treat, especially when topped with fresh berries.

Greek Yogurt Coleslaw

Ingredients:

For the Coleslaw:

- 1 small green cabbage, finely shredded
- 2 medium carrots, grated
- 1/2 cup red onion, thinly sliced

For the Dressing:

- 1 cup Greek yogurt (full-fat or low-fat)
- 2 tablespoons mayonnaise
- 2 tablespoons apple cider vinegar
- 1 tablespoon Dijon mustard
- 1 tablespoon honey
- Salt and black pepper to taste

Optional Add-ins:

- Chopped fresh parsley or cilantro for garnish
- Sunflower seeds or chopped nuts for crunch

Instructions:

Prepare the Vegetables:
- In a large bowl, combine the finely shredded green cabbage, grated carrots, and thinly sliced red onion.

Make the Dressing:
- In a separate bowl, whisk together the Greek yogurt, mayonnaise, apple cider vinegar, Dijon mustard, honey, salt, and black pepper until the dressing is smooth and well combined.

Combine Dressing with Vegetables:
- Pour the dressing over the shredded vegetables and toss until the coleslaw is evenly coated.

Refrigerate:
- Cover the bowl and refrigerate the Greek Yogurt Coleslaw for at least 1 hour before serving to allow the flavors to meld.

Adjust Seasoning:

- Before serving, taste the coleslaw and adjust the seasoning if needed. Add more salt, pepper, or vinegar according to your preference.

Garnish (Optional):
- Garnish with chopped fresh parsley or cilantro for a burst of freshness.

Optional Crunchy Toppings:
- For added crunch, sprinkle sunflower seeds or chopped nuts over the coleslaw before serving.

Serve:
- Serve the Greek Yogurt Coleslaw as a refreshing side dish with your favorite grilled meats, sandwiches, or as a topping for tacos.

This coleslaw is a healthier version of the classic, with the creamy Greek yogurt dressing providing a tangy and delicious twist. It's a versatile side dish that complements a variety of meals.

Greek Yogurt Pesto Pasta

Ingredients:

- 8 oz (about 225g) pasta (spaghetti, fettuccine, or your choice)
- 1 cup fresh basil leaves, packed
- 1/2 cup grated Parmesan cheese
- 1/4 cup pine nuts or walnuts
- 2 cloves garlic, minced
- 1/2 cup extra virgin olive oil
- 1 cup Greek yogurt (full-fat or low-fat)
- Salt and black pepper to taste
- Optional: Cherry tomatoes, sliced olives, or grilled chicken for garnish

Instructions:

Cook the Pasta:
- Cook the pasta according to the package instructions until al dente. Drain and set aside.

Make the Pesto Sauce:
- In a food processor, combine the fresh basil, grated Parmesan cheese, pine nuts or walnuts, and minced garlic. Pulse until the ingredients are finely chopped.

Add Olive Oil:
- With the food processor running, gradually add the extra virgin olive oil in a steady stream until the mixture forms a smooth pesto sauce.

Combine with Greek Yogurt:
- Transfer the pesto sauce to a bowl and stir in the Greek yogurt until well combined.

Season:
- Season the sauce with salt and black pepper to taste. Adjust the seasoning as needed.

Combine with Pasta:
- Pour the Greek Yogurt Pesto Sauce over the cooked pasta and toss until the pasta is evenly coated with the sauce.

Garnish (Optional):
- Garnish with cherry tomatoes, sliced olives, or grilled chicken if desired.

Serve:

- Serve the Greek Yogurt Pesto Pasta immediately, and enjoy the creamy and flavorful twist on traditional pesto pasta.

This Greek Yogurt Pesto Pasta offers a lighter and creamier alternative to classic pesto dishes. The addition of Greek yogurt adds a delightful tanginess and creamy texture, making it a delicious and satisfying meal.

Greek Yogurt and Herb Grilled Chicken

Ingredients:

- 4 boneless, skinless chicken breasts
- 1 cup Greek yogurt (full-fat or low-fat)
- 3 tablespoons extra virgin olive oil
- 3 cloves garlic, minced
- 2 tablespoons fresh lemon juice
- 1 tablespoon dried oregano
- 1 tablespoon fresh rosemary, chopped
- 1 teaspoon dried thyme
- Salt and black pepper to taste
- Lemon wedges for serving

Instructions:

Prepare Marinade:
- In a bowl, combine Greek yogurt, olive oil, minced garlic, lemon juice, dried oregano, fresh rosemary, dried thyme, salt, and black pepper. Mix well to create the marinade.

Marinate Chicken:
- Place the chicken breasts in a resealable plastic bag or shallow dish. Pour the Greek yogurt marinade over the chicken, ensuring each piece is well-coated. Seal the bag or cover the dish and refrigerate for at least 2 hours, or preferably overnight, to allow the flavors to infuse.

Preheat Grill:
- Preheat your grill to medium-high heat.

Remove Chicken from Marinade:
- Remove the chicken from the marinade, allowing any excess to drip off.

Grill Chicken:
- Grill the chicken breasts for approximately 6-8 minutes per side or until the internal temperature reaches 165°F (74°C) and the chicken is cooked through with nice grill marks.

Rest and Serve:
- Allow the grilled chicken to rest for a few minutes before slicing.

Serve with Lemon Wedges:

- Serve the Greek Yogurt and Herb Grilled Chicken slices with lemon wedges on the side for an extra burst of freshness.

Optional: Garnish with Fresh Herbs:
- Garnish the grilled chicken with additional fresh herbs, such as chopped parsley or rosemary, for a vibrant finish.

Enjoy this flavorful and juicy Greek Yogurt and Herb Grilled Chicken as a main dish, paired with your favorite sides or a fresh salad. The Greek yogurt marinade adds a creamy texture and enhances the herb-infused taste of the chicken.

Greek Yogurt Fruit Salad

Ingredients:

For the Fruit Salad:

- 2 cups fresh strawberries, hulled and halved
- 1 cup fresh blueberries
- 1 cup fresh pineapple, diced
- 1 cup grapes, halved
- 2 kiwi, peeled and sliced
- 1 banana, sliced
- 1 orange, peeled and segmented

For the Greek Yogurt Dressing:

- 1 cup Greek yogurt (full-fat or low-fat)
- 2 tablespoons honey
- 1 teaspoon vanilla extract
- Zest of 1 lemon
- Fresh mint leaves for garnish (optional)

Instructions:

Prepare the Fruit:
- In a large bowl, combine the strawberries, blueberries, pineapple, grapes, kiwi, banana, and orange segments. Gently toss the fruits together.

Make the Greek Yogurt Dressing:
- In a separate bowl, whisk together the Greek yogurt, honey, vanilla extract, and lemon zest until well combined.

Combine Dressing with Fruit:
- Pour the Greek yogurt dressing over the mixed fruits and gently toss until all the fruits are coated with the creamy dressing.

Chill:
- Cover the bowl and refrigerate the Greek Yogurt Fruit Salad for at least 30 minutes to allow the flavors to meld.

Garnish (Optional):
- Before serving, garnish the fruit salad with fresh mint leaves for a pop of color and extra freshness.

Serve:
- Serve the Greek Yogurt Fruit Salad as a refreshing and healthy dessert or snack.

This Greek Yogurt Fruit Salad is not only delicious but also packed with vitamins and antioxidants. The creamy Greek yogurt dressing adds a delightful touch to the vibrant mix of fresh fruits. Enjoy it on its own or as a side dish for breakfast or brunch.

Greek Yogurt and Avocado Dip

Ingredients:

- 1 ripe avocado, peeled and pitted
- 1 cup Greek yogurt (full-fat or low-fat)
- 1 clove garlic, minced
- 2 tablespoons fresh cilantro or parsley, chopped
- 1 tablespoon lime or lemon juice
- Salt and black pepper to taste
- Optional: 1/4 teaspoon cumin for extra flavor
- Optional: Red pepper flakes for a hint of spice

Instructions:

Prepare the Avocado:
- In a bowl, mash the ripe avocado with a fork until smooth.

Combine Ingredients:
- Add Greek yogurt, minced garlic, chopped cilantro or parsley, lime or lemon juice, and optional cumin to the mashed avocado. Mix well.

Season:
- Season the dip with salt and black pepper to taste. Adjust the seasoning according to your preference.

Optional Spice:
- If you like a bit of spice, add red pepper flakes to the dip and stir to combine.

Chill (Optional):
- For enhanced flavors, you can refrigerate the Greek Yogurt and Avocado Dip for about 30 minutes before serving.

Serve:
- Serve the dip with vegetable sticks, pita bread, tortilla chips, or as a topping for grilled chicken or fish.

Garnish (Optional):
- Garnish with additional chopped cilantro or parsley before serving.

This creamy and flavorful Greek Yogurt and Avocado Dip is a versatile and healthy option for snacking or as a dip for various dishes. It's rich in nutrients and offers a delightful combination of creamy avocado and tangy Greek yogurt.

Greek Yogurt Tandoori Chicken Skewers

Ingredients:

For the Marinade:

- 1 cup Greek yogurt (full-fat or low-fat)
- 2 tablespoons tandoori spice blend
- 1 tablespoon ground cumin
- 1 tablespoon ground coriander
- 1 tablespoon paprika
- 1 tablespoon ginger, minced
- 2 cloves garlic, minced
- 1 tablespoon lemon juice
- 1 teaspoon turmeric powder
- Salt and black pepper to taste

For the Chicken:

- 1.5 lbs (about 680g) boneless, skinless chicken thighs, cut into bite-sized pieces
- Olive oil for brushing

For Serving (Optional):

- Fresh cilantro, chopped
- Lemon wedges
- Greek yogurt for dipping

Instructions:

Prepare the Marinade:
- In a bowl, combine Greek yogurt, tandoori spice blend, ground cumin, ground coriander, paprika, minced ginger, minced garlic, lemon juice, turmeric powder, salt, and black pepper. Mix well to create the marinade.

Marinate the Chicken:

- Add the chicken pieces to the marinade, ensuring they are well-coated. Cover and refrigerate for at least 2 hours, or preferably overnight, to allow the flavors to penetrate the chicken.

Preheat the Grill:
- Preheat your grill or grill pan to medium-high heat.

Skewer the Chicken:
- Thread the marinated chicken pieces onto skewers.

Brush with Olive Oil:
- Brush the skewered chicken with olive oil to prevent sticking and promote even cooking.

Grill the Chicken Skewers:
- Grill the chicken skewers for approximately 12-15 minutes, turning occasionally, until the chicken is fully cooked and has a nice char.

Check for Doneness:
- Ensure the internal temperature of the chicken reaches 165°F (74°C).

Serve:
- Transfer the Greek Yogurt Tandoori Chicken Skewers to a serving platter.

Garnish (Optional):
- Garnish with chopped fresh cilantro and serve with lemon wedges and extra Greek yogurt for dipping.

Enjoy:
- Enjoy these flavorful Tandoori Chicken Skewers as a delicious and protein-packed appetizer or main dish.

This recipe combines the classic flavors of tandoori with the creamy richness of Greek yogurt, resulting in tender and flavorful chicken skewers. It's a perfect dish for grilling and sharing with family and friends.

Greek Yogurt Caesar Salad

Ingredients:

For the Caesar Dressing:

- 1 cup Greek yogurt (full-fat or low-fat)
- 2 tablespoons mayonnaise
- 2 tablespoons Dijon mustard
- 2 cloves garlic, minced
- 2 anchovy fillets, minced (optional)
- 2 tablespoons grated Parmesan cheese
- 1 tablespoon lemon juice
- 1 teaspoon Worcestershire sauce
- Salt and black pepper to taste

For the Salad:

- Romaine lettuce, washed and chopped
- Croutons (store-bought or homemade)
- Grated Parmesan cheese for topping
- Optional: Grilled chicken breast or shrimp for protein

Instructions:

Prepare the Caesar Dressing:
- In a bowl, whisk together Greek yogurt, mayonnaise, Dijon mustard, minced garlic, minced anchovy fillets (if using), grated Parmesan cheese, lemon juice, Worcestershire sauce, salt, and black pepper. Mix well until smooth and creamy.

Assemble the Salad:
- In a large salad bowl, toss the chopped Romaine lettuce with the desired amount of Caesar dressing. Coat the lettuce evenly.

Add Croutons:
- Add croutons to the salad for crunch. You can use store-bought croutons or make your own by toasting cubes of bread with olive oil and herbs.

Optional Protein:
- For an extra protein boost, add grilled chicken breast or shrimp to the salad.

Top with Parmesan Cheese:
- Sprinkle grated Parmesan cheese over the salad.

Toss and Serve:
- Toss the salad ingredients together until well combined.

Serve Immediately:
- Serve the Greek Yogurt Caesar Salad immediately, garnished with additional Parmesan cheese if desired.

Enjoy:
- Enjoy this healthier version of Caesar salad with the creamy goodness of Greek yogurt.

This Greek Yogurt Caesar Salad offers a lighter take on the classic Caesar, with the rich and creamy dressing made using Greek yogurt. It's a satisfying and flavorful salad that can be enjoyed as a side dish or as a complete meal with added protein.

Greek Yogurt Chicken Gyros

Ingredients:

For the Chicken Marinade:

- 1.5 lbs (about 680g) boneless, skinless chicken thighs, thinly sliced
- 1 cup Greek yogurt (full-fat or low-fat)
- 3 tablespoons olive oil
- 3 cloves garlic, minced
- 1 tablespoon dried oregano
- 1 tablespoon smoked paprika
- 1 teaspoon ground cumin
- 1 teaspoon ground coriander
- Salt and black pepper to taste
- Juice of 1 lemon

For the Tzatziki Sauce:

- 1 cup Greek yogurt (full-fat or low-fat)
- 1 cucumber, grated and squeezed to remove excess moisture
- 2 cloves garlic, minced
- 1 tablespoon fresh dill, chopped
- 1 tablespoon extra virgin olive oil
- Salt and black pepper to taste
- Juice of 1/2 lemon

For Serving:

- Pita bread or flatbreads
- Sliced tomatoes
- Sliced red onions
- Lettuce leaves
- Feta cheese, crumbled (optional)

Instructions:

Prepare the Chicken Marinade:

- In a bowl, combine Greek yogurt, olive oil, minced garlic, dried oregano, smoked paprika, ground cumin, ground coriander, salt, black pepper, and lemon juice. Mix well.

Marinate the Chicken:
- Add the thinly sliced chicken thighs to the marinade, ensuring they are well-coated. Cover and refrigerate for at least 2 hours, or preferably overnight.

Make the Tzatziki Sauce:
- In a separate bowl, combine Greek yogurt, grated cucumber, minced garlic, chopped fresh dill, olive oil, salt, black pepper, and lemon juice. Mix well and refrigerate until ready to use.

Cook the Chicken:
- Heat a grill or grill pan over medium-high heat. Grill the marinated chicken slices for about 5-7 minutes per side or until fully cooked and slightly charred.

Warm the Pita Bread:
- Warm the pita bread or flatbreads on the grill or in a pan.

Assemble the Gyros:
- Spread a generous amount of Tzatziki sauce on each warmed pita bread. Place grilled chicken slices on top.

Add Toppings:
- Add sliced tomatoes, sliced red onions, lettuce leaves, and crumbled feta cheese if desired.

Fold and Serve:
- Fold the pita bread to create a gyro and secure it with a toothpick. Serve immediately.

Enjoy:
- Enjoy these delicious and flavorful Greek Yogurt Chicken Gyros as a satisfying meal.

These homemade gyros are a healthier version with the creamy Greek yogurt marinade and tzatziki sauce. They make for a delicious and satisfying meal, perfect for lunch or dinner.

Greek Yogurt Ranch Chicken Wings

Ingredients:

For the Chicken Wings:

- 2 lbs (about 907g) chicken wings, split at joints, tips discarded
- 1 cup Greek yogurt (full-fat or low-fat)
- 3 tablespoons olive oil
- 3 cloves garlic, minced
- 1 tablespoon dried oregano
- 1 tablespoon dried parsley
- 1 teaspoon onion powder
- 1 teaspoon garlic powder
- Salt and black pepper to taste

For the Ranch Dip:

- 1 cup Greek yogurt (full-fat or low-fat)
- 1 tablespoon dried dill
- 1 tablespoon dried chives
- 1 teaspoon garlic powder
- 1 teaspoon onion powder
- Salt and black pepper to taste

Instructions:

Preheat the Oven:
- Preheat your oven to 400°F (200°C).

Prepare the Chicken Wings:
- In a large bowl, mix together Greek yogurt, olive oil, minced garlic, dried oregano, dried parsley, onion powder, garlic powder, salt, and black pepper to create the marinade.

Coat the Wings:
- Add the chicken wings to the bowl and toss until the wings are evenly coated with the Greek yogurt marinade.

Marinate:

- Allow the wings to marinate in the refrigerator for at least 1 hour, or preferably overnight, to enhance the flavors.

Bake the Wings:
- Place the marinated chicken wings on a baking sheet lined with parchment paper. Bake in the preheated oven for 40-45 minutes or until the wings are golden brown and cooked through.

Prepare the Ranch Dip:
- While the wings are baking, prepare the Ranch dip by mixing Greek yogurt, dried dill, dried chives, garlic powder, onion powder, salt, and black pepper in a bowl.

Serve:
- Once the wings are done, serve them hot with the prepared Greek Yogurt Ranch dip on the side.

Garnish (Optional):
- Garnish the wings with additional dried herbs for a fresh and herby touch.

Enjoy:
- Enjoy these Greek Yogurt Ranch Chicken Wings as a tasty and healthier alternative to traditional wings.

These chicken wings are not only delicious but also provide a healthier twist with the Greek yogurt marinade. Paired with the homemade Greek Yogurt Ranch dip, they make for a flavorful and satisfying appetizer or main course.

Greek Yogurt and Berry Popsicles

Ingredients:

- 1 cup Greek yogurt (full-fat or low-fat)
- 1 cup mixed berries (strawberries, blueberries, raspberries)
- 2 tablespoons honey or maple syrup
- 1 teaspoon vanilla extract
- Optional: Fresh mint leaves for garnish

Instructions:

Prepare the Berry Mixture:
- In a blender or food processor, combine the mixed berries, honey (or maple syrup), and vanilla extract. Blend until you have a smooth berry mixture.

Layer the Popsicles:
- Spoon a small amount of the berry mixture into the bottom of each popsicle mold, filling them about one-third of the way.

Add Greek Yogurt Layer:
- Add a layer of Greek yogurt on top of the berry mixture, filling another one-third of the mold.

Repeat Layers:
- Repeat the process, alternating between the berry mixture and Greek yogurt until the molds are filled.

Create Swirls (Optional):
- Use a skewer or popsicle stick to gently swirl the layers together, creating a marbled effect.

Insert Popsicle Sticks:
- Insert popsicle sticks into the molds.

Freeze:
- Place the popsicle mold in the freezer and let the popsicles freeze for at least 4-6 hours or until solid.

Unmold and Serve:
- Once fully frozen, run the popsicle mold under warm water for a few seconds to loosen the popsicles. Carefully unmold the popsicles.

Garnish (Optional):
- Garnish with fresh mint leaves for a burst of freshness.

Enjoy:

- Enjoy these delicious and refreshing Greek Yogurt and Berry Popsicles on a hot day or as a healthy dessert.

These homemade popsicles are not only a delightful treat but also a healthier alternative with the addition of Greek yogurt. They are perfect for cooling down during the warmer months while providing a burst of fruity and creamy goodness.

Greek Yogurt Veggie Dip

Ingredients:

- 1 cup Greek yogurt (full-fat or low-fat)
- 1/2 cup mayonnaise
- 1 tablespoon lemon juice
- 1 teaspoon Dijon mustard
- 2 cloves garlic, minced
- 1 teaspoon dried dill
- 1 teaspoon dried parsley
- 1/2 teaspoon onion powder
- Salt and black pepper to taste
- Assorted fresh vegetables for dipping (carrots, cucumber, bell peppers, cherry tomatoes, etc.)

Instructions:

Prepare the Dip:
- In a bowl, combine Greek yogurt, mayonnaise, lemon juice, Dijon mustard, minced garlic, dried dill, dried parsley, onion powder, salt, and black pepper. Mix well until all ingredients are thoroughly combined.

Adjust Seasoning:
- Taste the dip and adjust the seasoning, adding more salt, pepper, or lemon juice according to your preference.

Chill:
- Cover the bowl and refrigerate the Greek Yogurt Veggie Dip for at least 1 hour before serving to allow the flavors to meld.

Prepare Vegetables:
- Wash, peel, and chop a variety of fresh vegetables for dipping. Carrot sticks, cucumber slices, bell pepper strips, and cherry tomatoes work well.

Serve:
- Transfer the chilled Greek Yogurt Veggie Dip to a serving bowl and place it in the center of a platter.

Arrange Vegetables:
- Arrange the prepared vegetable sticks and slices around the dip on the platter.

Garnish (Optional):

- Garnish the dip with a sprinkle of dried dill or parsley for a decorative touch.

Enjoy:
- Enjoy this creamy and flavorful Greek Yogurt Veggie Dip with a variety of fresh vegetables as a healthy and delicious snack or appetizer.

This veggie dip, made with Greek yogurt, adds a creamy and tangy twist to your favorite fresh vegetables. It's a perfect choice for parties, gatherings, or as a wholesome snack any time of the day.

Greek Yogurt Chicken Curry

Ingredients:

For the Chicken Marinade:

- 1.5 lbs (about 680g) boneless, skinless chicken thighs, cut into bite-sized pieces
- 1 cup Greek yogurt (full-fat or low-fat)
- 2 tablespoons olive oil
- 1 tablespoon ginger paste
- 1 tablespoon garlic paste
- 1 teaspoon turmeric powder
- 1 teaspoon ground cumin
- 1 teaspoon ground coriander
- 1 teaspoon chili powder (adjust to taste)
- Salt and black pepper to taste

For the Curry:

- 2 tablespoons vegetable oil
- 1 large onion, finely chopped
- 2 tomatoes, pureed
- 1 cup Greek yogurt (full-fat or low-fat)
- 1 teaspoon ground cumin
- 1 teaspoon ground coriander
- 1 teaspoon garam masala
- 1/2 teaspoon turmeric powder
- 1/2 teaspoon chili powder (adjust to taste)
- Salt to taste
- Fresh cilantro, chopped, for garnish

Instructions:

Marinate the Chicken:
- In a bowl, combine the chicken pieces with Greek yogurt, olive oil, ginger paste, garlic paste, turmeric powder, ground cumin, ground coriander, chili powder, salt, and black pepper. Mix well and let it marinate for at least 30 minutes, or preferably, overnight in the refrigerator.

Cook the Chicken:

- Heat vegetable oil in a large pan over medium heat. Add the marinated chicken and cook until browned on all sides and cooked through. Remove the chicken from the pan and set aside.

Prepare the Curry Base:
- In the same pan, add a bit more oil if needed. Add finely chopped onion and sauté until golden brown.

Add Spices:
- Stir in ground cumin, ground coriander, turmeric powder, and chili powder. Cook for a minute until the spices release their aroma.

Add Tomato Puree:
- Add the pureed tomatoes to the pan and cook until the oil starts to separate from the tomato mixture.

Combine Yogurt:
- Lower the heat and gradually add Greek yogurt to the tomato mixture, stirring continuously to avoid curdling.

Return Chicken to the Pan:
- Return the cooked chicken to the pan, coating it with the yogurt and tomato mixture.

Simmer:
- Add garam masala and salt to taste. Simmer the curry on low heat for 15-20 minutes, allowing the flavors to meld.

Garnish and Serve:
- Garnish with fresh cilantro and serve the Greek Yogurt Chicken Curry hot with rice or naan.

This Greek Yogurt Chicken Curry is a creamy and flavorful twist on traditional curry. The Greek yogurt adds a rich and tangy element to the dish, creating a delicious and satisfying meal.

Greek Yogurt and Herb Quinoa Salad

Ingredients:

For the Salad:

- 1 cup quinoa, rinsed and cooked according to package instructions
- 1 cup cherry tomatoes, halved
- 1 cucumber, diced
- 1/2 red onion, finely chopped
- 1/2 cup Kalamata olives, sliced
- 1/2 cup feta cheese, crumbled
- Fresh parsley, chopped, for garnish

For the Greek Yogurt Dressing:

- 1 cup Greek yogurt (full-fat or low-fat)
- 2 tablespoons extra virgin olive oil
- 2 tablespoons lemon juice
- 2 cloves garlic, minced
- 1 teaspoon dried oregano
- Salt and black pepper to taste

Instructions:

Prepare Quinoa:
- Rinse quinoa under cold water and cook according to the package instructions. Allow it to cool.

Make the Greek Yogurt Dressing:
- In a bowl, whisk together Greek yogurt, olive oil, lemon juice, minced garlic, dried oregano, salt, and black pepper until well combined. Adjust seasoning to taste.

Assemble the Salad:
- In a large mixing bowl, combine the cooked quinoa, cherry tomatoes, diced cucumber, chopped red onion, sliced Kalamata olives, and crumbled feta cheese.

Add Greek Yogurt Dressing:

- Pour the Greek Yogurt Dressing over the salad and toss until all ingredients are well-coated.

Garnish:
- Garnish the Greek Yogurt and Herb Quinoa Salad with fresh parsley.

Chill (Optional):
- For enhanced flavors, you can refrigerate the salad for about 30 minutes before serving.

Serve:
- Serve the salad chilled or at room temperature as a refreshing and nutritious side dish or a light main course.

This Greek Yogurt and Herb Quinoa Salad combines the goodness of quinoa with a creamy Greek yogurt dressing, creating a flavorful and satisfying dish. It's perfect for a healthy lunch, dinner, or as a side for picnics and gatherings.

Greek Yogurt Lemon Bars

Ingredients:

For the Crust:

- 1 cup all-purpose flour
- 1/2 cup unsalted butter, softened
- 1/4 cup powdered sugar
- Pinch of salt

For the Filling:

- 1 cup Greek yogurt (full-fat or low-fat)
- 1 cup granulated sugar
- 3 large eggs
- 1/2 cup fresh lemon juice
- 2 tablespoons lemon zest
- 1/4 cup all-purpose flour
- 1/2 teaspoon baking powder
- Powdered sugar for dusting (optional)

Instructions:

Preheat the Oven:
- Preheat your oven to 350°F (175°C) and grease a 9x9-inch baking dish.

Prepare the Crust:
- In a mixing bowl, combine the softened butter, all-purpose flour, powdered sugar, and a pinch of salt. Mix until the ingredients come together to form a crumbly dough.

Press into Baking Dish:
- Press the crust mixture into the bottom of the greased baking dish to form an even layer. Bake in the preheated oven for about 15-18 minutes or until the edges are lightly golden. Allow the crust to cool while preparing the filling.

Make the Filling:
- In a separate bowl, whisk together Greek yogurt, granulated sugar, eggs, fresh lemon juice, lemon zest, all-purpose flour, and baking powder until well combined.

Pour over Crust:
- Pour the lemon filling over the pre-baked crust, spreading it evenly.

Bake:
- Bake in the oven for approximately 25-30 minutes or until the edges are set, and the center is slightly firm.

Cool and Chill:
- Allow the Greek Yogurt Lemon Bars to cool in the baking dish, then refrigerate for at least 2 hours or until fully chilled.

Dust with Powdered Sugar (Optional):
- Before serving, you can dust the chilled lemon bars with powdered sugar for a decorative touch.

Slice and Serve:
- Cut into squares and serve these delightful Greek Yogurt Lemon Bars as a refreshing and tangy dessert.

These Greek Yogurt Lemon Bars offer a creamy and citrusy twist on the classic dessert. The addition of Greek yogurt not only adds a delightful tang but also creates a smooth and luscious texture. Enjoy these bars as a sweet treat for any occasion.

Greek Yogurt Chicken Tzatziki Wrap

Ingredients:

For the Greek Yogurt Marinated Chicken:

- 1 lb (about 450g) boneless, skinless chicken breasts or thighs
- 1 cup Greek yogurt (full-fat or low-fat)
- 3 tablespoons olive oil
- 2 tablespoons lemon juice
- 2 cloves garlic, minced
- 1 teaspoon dried oregano
- 1 teaspoon dried thyme
- Salt and black pepper to taste

For the Tzatziki Sauce:

- 1 cup Greek yogurt (full-fat or low-fat)
- 1 cucumber, finely diced
- 2 cloves garlic, minced
- 1 tablespoon fresh dill, chopped
- 1 tablespoon extra virgin olive oil
- 1 tablespoon lemon juice
- Salt and black pepper to taste

For the Wrap:

- Whole wheat or spinach wraps
- Cherry tomatoes, sliced
- Red onion, thinly sliced
- Lettuce leaves
- Feta cheese, crumbled (optional)

Instructions:

    Marinate the Chicken:

- In a bowl, combine Greek yogurt, olive oil, lemon juice, minced garlic, dried oregano, dried thyme, salt, and black pepper. Mix well. Add the chicken to the marinade, ensuring it's well-coated. Marinate for at least 30 minutes, or preferably, overnight.

Cook the Chicken:
- Preheat a grill or grill pan over medium-high heat. Grill the marinated chicken until fully cooked, about 6-8 minutes per side. Let it rest for a few minutes before slicing.

Prepare Tzatziki Sauce:
- In a bowl, combine Greek yogurt, finely diced cucumber, minced garlic, chopped fresh dill, olive oil, lemon juice, salt, and black pepper. Mix well to create the tzatziki sauce.

Assemble the Wrap:
- Spread a generous amount of tzatziki sauce on a whole wheat or spinach wrap.

Add Chicken and Vegetables:
- Place sliced Greek Yogurt Marinated Chicken on the wrap. Add sliced cherry tomatoes, thinly sliced red onion, lettuce leaves, and crumbled feta cheese if desired.

Wrap and Serve:
- Fold the sides of the wrap and roll it tightly. Secure with a toothpick if needed. Cut in half diagonally.

Enjoy:
- Serve the Greek Yogurt Chicken Tzatziki Wrap immediately and enjoy a delicious and wholesome Mediterranean-inspired meal.

This Greek Yogurt Chicken Tzatziki Wrap is a flavorful and satisfying option for a quick and healthy lunch or dinner. The Greek yogurt-marinated chicken and creamy tzatziki sauce add a burst of Mediterranean flavors to the wrap.

Greek Yogurt Hummus

Ingredients:

- 1 can (15 ounces) chickpeas, drained and rinsed
- 1/4 cup tahini
- 1/4 cup Greek yogurt (full-fat or low-fat)
- 3 tablespoons extra virgin olive oil
- 2 cloves garlic, minced
- 1 teaspoon ground cumin
- 1/2 teaspoon smoked paprika
- Juice of 1 lemon
- Salt and black pepper to taste
- Water (as needed for desired consistency)
- Optional garnish: Extra virgin olive oil, paprika, chopped fresh parsley

Instructions:

Prepare Chickpeas:
- Drain and rinse the chickpeas under cold water.

Combine Ingredients:
- In a food processor, combine chickpeas, tahini, Greek yogurt, extra virgin olive oil, minced garlic, ground cumin, smoked paprika, lemon juice, salt, and black pepper.

Blend:
- Blend the ingredients until smooth. If the hummus is too thick, you can add water, one tablespoon at a time, until you achieve your desired consistency.

Adjust Seasoning:
- Taste the hummus and adjust the seasoning, adding more salt, pepper, or lemon juice if needed.

Serve:
- Transfer the Greek Yogurt Hummus to a serving bowl.

Garnish (Optional):
- Drizzle with extra virgin olive oil, sprinkle with smoked paprika, and garnish with chopped fresh parsley.

Enjoy:
- Serve the Greek Yogurt Hummus with pita bread, fresh vegetables, or as a spread for sandwiches and wraps.

This Greek Yogurt Hummus is a creamy and tangy twist on the classic hummus recipe. The addition of Greek yogurt enhances the texture and adds a delightful richness. Enjoy it as a healthy dip or spread for a variety of dishes.

Greek Yogurt Raspberry Tart

Ingredients:

For the Tart Crust:

- 1 1/2 cups almond flour
- 1/4 cup coconut flour
- 1/4 cup melted coconut oil
- 2 tablespoons maple syrup or honey
- 1 teaspoon vanilla extract
- Pinch of salt

For the Greek Yogurt Filling:

- 2 cups Greek yogurt (full-fat or low-fat)
- 1/4 cup honey or maple syrup (adjust to taste)
- 1 teaspoon vanilla extract

For the Raspberry Topping:

- 2 cups fresh raspberries
- 1-2 tablespoons honey for drizzling (optional)
- Mint leaves for garnish (optional)

Instructions:

Preheat the Oven:
- Preheat your oven to 350°F (175°C).

Prepare the Tart Crust:
- In a bowl, combine almond flour, coconut flour, melted coconut oil, maple syrup or honey, vanilla extract, and a pinch of salt. Mix until a crumbly dough forms.

Press into Tart Pan:
- Press the dough evenly into the bottom and up the sides of a tart pan with a removable bottom.

Bake the Crust:

- Bake the tart crust in the preheated oven for about 10-12 minutes or until it's golden brown. Allow it to cool completely.

Prepare the Greek Yogurt Filling:
- In a bowl, mix Greek yogurt, honey or maple syrup, and vanilla extract until well combined.

Fill the Tart:
- Spread the Greek Yogurt Filling evenly over the cooled tart crust.

Arrange Raspberries:
- Arrange fresh raspberries on top of the Greek Yogurt Filling.

Drizzle with Honey (Optional):
- If desired, drizzle honey over the raspberries for added sweetness.

Chill:
- Refrigerate the Greek Yogurt Raspberry Tart for at least 2 hours to allow the filling to set.

Garnish and Serve:
- Before serving, garnish with mint leaves if desired. Slice and serve chilled.

Enjoy:
- Enjoy this refreshing and delightful Greek Yogurt Raspberry Tart as a healthy dessert or treat.

This Greek Yogurt Raspberry Tart is not only visually appealing but also a delicious and nutritious dessert option. The almond flour crust adds a nutty flavor, while the Greek yogurt filling provides a creamy and tangy balance to the sweetness of fresh raspberries.

Greek Yogurt and Cucumber Gazpacho

Ingredients:

- 2 large cucumbers, peeled and diced
- 1 green bell pepper, chopped
- 1 small red onion, chopped
- 3 cups Greek yogurt (full-fat or low-fat)
- 2 cloves garlic, minced
- 1/4 cup fresh dill, chopped
- 1/4 cup fresh mint, chopped
- 3 tablespoons extra virgin olive oil
- 2 tablespoons red wine vinegar
- Salt and black pepper to taste
- 1 cup cold water (optional, for thinning)
- Optional garnish: Greek yogurt, diced cucumber, fresh herbs

Instructions:

Prepare Vegetables:
- Peel and dice the cucumbers. Chop the green bell pepper and red onion.

Blend Vegetables:
- In a blender or food processor, combine the diced cucumbers, chopped bell pepper, red onion, minced garlic, fresh dill, and fresh mint. Blend until smooth.

Add Greek Yogurt:
- Add Greek yogurt to the blended vegetables and continue blending until well combined.

Incorporate Olive Oil and Vinegar:
- With the blender running, slowly drizzle in the extra virgin olive oil and red wine vinegar until the gazpacho reaches your desired consistency.

Season:
- Season the gazpacho with salt and black pepper to taste. Adjust the seasoning as needed.

Chill:
- Refrigerate the gazpacho for at least 2 hours or until well chilled.

Thin with Water (Optional):

- If the gazpacho is too thick, you can thin it with cold water to achieve the desired consistency.

Serve:
- Ladle the Greek Yogurt and Cucumber Gazpacho into bowls. If desired, garnish with a dollop of Greek yogurt, diced cucumber, and fresh herbs.

Enjoy:
- Serve this refreshing and creamy gazpacho as a chilled soup on a hot day or as a light appetizer.

This Greek Yogurt and Cucumber Gazpacho is a cool and refreshing twist on the classic gazpacho soup. The addition of Greek yogurt adds creaminess and a hint of tanginess, making it a delightful summer dish.

Greek Yogurt and Herb Stuffed Mushrooms

Ingredients:

- 20 large mushrooms, cleaned and stems removed
- 1 cup Greek yogurt (full-fat or low-fat)
- 1/2 cup feta cheese, crumbled
- 1/4 cup grated Parmesan cheese
- 2 cloves garlic, minced
- 2 tablespoons fresh parsley, chopped
- 1 tablespoon fresh dill, chopped
- 1 tablespoon fresh chives, chopped
- 2 tablespoons olive oil
- Salt and black pepper to taste
- Optional: Panko breadcrumbs for topping

Instructions:

Prepare the Mushrooms:
- Preheat the oven to 375°F (190°C). Clean the mushrooms and remove the stems. Place the mushroom caps on a baking sheet lined with parchment paper.

Make the Filling:
- In a bowl, combine Greek yogurt, crumbled feta cheese, grated Parmesan cheese, minced garlic, chopped parsley, chopped dill, chopped chives, olive oil, salt, and black pepper. Mix well.

Fill the Mushrooms:
- Spoon the Greek yogurt and herb filling into each mushroom cap, pressing it down gently.

Optional Topping:
- If desired, sprinkle a small amount of Panko breadcrumbs on top of each stuffed mushroom for added crunch.

Bake:
- Bake the stuffed mushrooms in the preheated oven for approximately 20-25 minutes or until the mushrooms are tender and the filling is golden brown.

Serve:

- Remove from the oven and let the stuffed mushrooms cool slightly before serving.

Garnish (Optional):
- Garnish with additional fresh herbs before serving if desired.

Enjoy:
- Serve these Greek Yogurt and Herb Stuffed Mushrooms as a delicious appetizer or party snack.

These stuffed mushrooms are not only flavorful but also packed with protein from the Greek yogurt and the richness of herbs. They make an excellent appetizer for gatherings or a tasty snack for any occasion.

Greek Yogurt and Honey Mustard Chicken

Ingredients:

- 4 boneless, skinless chicken breasts
- 1 cup Greek yogurt (full-fat or low-fat)
- 3 tablespoons Dijon mustard
- 2 tablespoons honey
- 2 cloves garlic, minced
- 1 teaspoon dried thyme
- 1 teaspoon dried rosemary
- Salt and black pepper to taste
- Fresh parsley for garnish (optional)

Instructions:

Preheat the Oven:
- Preheat your oven to 375°F (190°C).

Prepare the Marinade:
- In a bowl, mix together Greek yogurt, Dijon mustard, honey, minced garlic, dried thyme, dried rosemary, salt, and black pepper.

Marinate the Chicken:
- Place the chicken breasts in a shallow dish or a resealable plastic bag. Pour half of the Greek yogurt marinade over the chicken, ensuring each piece is well-coated. Reserve the remaining marinade for later.

Marinate Time:
- Allow the chicken to marinate in the refrigerator for at least 30 minutes. For more flavor, you can marinate it for up to 24 hours.

Cook the Chicken:
- Place the marinated chicken breasts on a baking sheet lined with parchment paper. Bake in the preheated oven for about 25-30 minutes or until the chicken is cooked through and reaches an internal temperature of 165°F (74°C).

Make Honey Mustard Sauce:
- While the chicken is baking, mix the reserved Greek yogurt marinade with additional honey and Dijon mustard to create a honey mustard sauce.

Serve:

- Once the chicken is done, drizzle the honey mustard sauce over the top. Garnish with fresh parsley if desired.

Enjoy:
- Serve the Greek Yogurt and Honey Mustard Chicken with your favorite sides for a delicious and creamy meal.

This Greek Yogurt and Honey Mustard Chicken recipe results in juicy and flavorful chicken breasts with a creamy and tangy sauce. The Greek yogurt marinade helps to keep the chicken moist while infusing it with a rich taste. It's a simple and tasty dish perfect for a weeknight dinner.

Greek Yogurt and Lemon Herb Salmon

Ingredients:

- 4 salmon fillets
- 1 cup Greek yogurt (full-fat or low-fat)
- Zest of 1 lemon
- Juice of 1 lemon
- 2 tablespoons fresh dill, chopped
- 1 tablespoon fresh parsley, chopped
- 2 cloves garlic, minced
- 1 tablespoon olive oil
- Salt and black pepper to taste
- Lemon slices for garnish

Instructions:

Preheat the Oven:
- Preheat your oven to 400°F (200°C).

Prepare the Greek Yogurt Marinade:
- In a bowl, mix together Greek yogurt, lemon zest, lemon juice, chopped dill, chopped parsley, minced garlic, olive oil, salt, and black pepper.

Marinate the Salmon:
- Place the salmon fillets in a baking dish or on a lined baking sheet. Spread the Greek yogurt marinade over each fillet, ensuring they are well-coated. Allow the salmon to marinate for at least 15-30 minutes.

Bake the Salmon:
- Bake the salmon in the preheated oven for about 15-20 minutes or until the fish is cooked through and flakes easily with a fork.

Broil for Crispy Top (Optional):
- If you desire a crispy top, you can turn on the broiler for the last 2-3 minutes of cooking until the top is golden brown.

Garnish:
- Garnish the Greek Yogurt and Lemon Herb Salmon with lemon slices and additional chopped herbs.

Serve:
- Serve the salmon hot with your favorite sides, such as roasted vegetables, quinoa, or a fresh salad.

Enjoy:
- Enjoy this flavorful and creamy Greek Yogurt and Lemon Herb Salmon as a delicious and nutritious main course.

This recipe combines the richness of Greek yogurt with the brightness of lemon and herbs to create a delightful marinade for salmon. The result is a juicy and flavorful dish that's easy to prepare for a healthy and satisfying meal.

Greek Yogurt and Berry Breakfast Pizza

Ingredients:

For the Pizza Dough:

- 2 1/4 cups all-purpose flour
- 1 tablespoon sugar
- 1 packet (2 1/4 teaspoons) active dry yeast
- 1 cup warm water (110°F/43°C)
- 1 tablespoon olive oil
- 1/2 teaspoon salt

For the Toppings:

- 1 1/2 cups Greek yogurt (full-fat or low-fat)
- 2 tablespoons honey
- 1 teaspoon vanilla extract
- Assorted berries (strawberries, blueberries, raspberries)
- 2 tablespoons sliced almonds (optional)
- Fresh mint leaves for garnish

Instructions:

Prepare the Pizza Dough:
- In a bowl, combine warm water, sugar, and active dry yeast. Let it sit for about 5 minutes until frothy.
- In a large mixing bowl, combine flour and salt. Make a well in the center and pour in the yeast mixture and olive oil.
- Mix until a dough forms. Knead the dough on a floured surface for about 5-7 minutes until smooth and elastic.
- Place the dough in a lightly oiled bowl, cover with a kitchen towel, and let it rise in a warm place for 1-2 hours or until it doubles in size.

Preheat the Oven:
- Preheat your oven to 475°F (245°C). If you have a pizza stone, place it in the oven while preheating.

Roll Out the Dough:
- Punch down the risen dough and roll it out on a floured surface into your desired pizza shape.

Bake the Dough:
- If using a pizza stone, transfer the rolled-out dough onto a piece of parchment paper. If not using a pizza stone, place the rolled-out dough on a baking sheet.
- Bake the dough in the preheated oven for 8-10 minutes or until it's golden brown and cooked through.

Prepare the Greek Yogurt Topping:
- In a bowl, mix Greek yogurt, honey, and vanilla extract until well combined.

Assemble the Breakfast Pizza:
- Once the pizza crust has cooled slightly, spread the Greek yogurt mixture evenly over the crust.
- Arrange assorted berries on top of the Greek yogurt. Sprinkle with sliced almonds if desired.

Garnish:
- Garnish the Greek Yogurt and Berry Breakfast Pizza with fresh mint leaves.

Slice and Serve:
- Slice the breakfast pizza into wedges and serve.

Enjoy:
- Enjoy this delicious and nutritious Greek Yogurt and Berry Breakfast Pizza as a delightful start to your day.

This breakfast pizza combines the creaminess of Greek yogurt with the sweetness of honey and fresh berries on a homemade crust, creating a tasty and satisfying morning treat.

Greek Yogurt and Cilantro Lime Rice

Ingredients:

- 1 cup long-grain white rice
- 2 cups water
- 1/2 cup Greek yogurt (full-fat or low-fat)
- Zest of 1 lime
- Juice of 1 lime
- 2 tablespoons fresh cilantro, chopped
- 1 tablespoon olive oil
- Salt to taste

Instructions:

Cook the Rice:
- Rinse the rice under cold water until the water runs clear. In a medium saucepan, bring 2 cups of water to a boil. Add the rice, reduce heat to low, cover, and simmer for 15-20 minutes or until the rice is cooked and water is absorbed.

Prepare the Greek Yogurt Mixture:
- In a bowl, mix Greek yogurt, lime zest, lime juice, chopped cilantro, olive oil, and salt.

Fluff the Rice:
- Once the rice is cooked, fluff it with a fork to separate the grains.

Combine with Greek Yogurt Mixture:
- While the rice is still warm, gently fold in the Greek yogurt mixture until well combined.

Adjust Seasoning:
- Taste and adjust the salt or lime juice if needed.

Serve:
- Serve the Greek Yogurt and Cilantro Lime Rice as a flavorful and creamy side dish.

Enjoy:
- Enjoy this tangy and herby rice alongside your favorite main dishes.

This Greek Yogurt and Cilantro Lime Rice is a refreshing and creamy twist on traditional cilantro lime rice. The addition of Greek yogurt adds a delightful tanginess, making it a perfect side dish for a variety of meals, especially those with a hint of Mediterranean or Mexican flavors.

Greek Yogurt Berry Popsicles

Ingredients:

- 1 cup Greek yogurt (full-fat or low-fat)
- 1 cup mixed berries (strawberries, blueberries, raspberries)
- 2 tablespoons honey or maple syrup (adjust to taste)
- 1 teaspoon vanilla extract
- Popsicle molds

Instructions:

Prepare the Greek Yogurt Mixture:
- In a blender or food processor, combine Greek yogurt, mixed berries, honey or maple syrup, and vanilla extract. Blend until smooth.

Adjust Sweetness:
- Taste the mixture and adjust the sweetness by adding more honey or maple syrup if needed.

Fill Popsicle Molds:
- Pour the Greek yogurt and berry mixture into popsicle molds, leaving a little space at the top for expansion.

Insert Sticks:
- Insert popsicle sticks into the center of each mold.

Freeze:
- Place the popsicle molds in the freezer and let them freeze for at least 4-6 hours or until completely solid.

Unmold and Serve:
- Once the popsicles are frozen, run the molds briefly under warm water to loosen the popsicles. Gently pull them out of the molds.

Enjoy:
- Serve these refreshing Greek Yogurt Berry Popsicles on a hot day as a healthy and delicious treat.

These Greek Yogurt Berry Popsicles are a delightful and wholesome way to enjoy the goodness of yogurt and fresh berries. They make a perfect summer snack or dessert for both kids and adults.

Greek Yogurt Chicken Fajitas

Ingredients:

For the Marinade:

- 1 pound boneless, skinless chicken breasts, sliced into strips
- 1 cup Greek yogurt (full-fat or low-fat)
- 2 tablespoons olive oil
- 2 tablespoons lime juice
- 2 teaspoons ground cumin
- 2 teaspoons chili powder
- 1 teaspoon paprika
- 1 teaspoon garlic powder
- Salt and black pepper to taste

For the Fajitas:

- 1 tablespoon olive oil
- 1 red bell pepper, sliced
- 1 green bell pepper, sliced
- 1 yellow onion, sliced
- Flour or corn tortillas
- Toppings: Greek yogurt, salsa, guacamole, shredded cheese, fresh cilantro

Instructions:

Prepare the Marinade:
- In a bowl, whisk together Greek yogurt, olive oil, lime juice, ground cumin, chili powder, paprika, garlic powder, salt, and black pepper to create the marinade.

Marinate the Chicken:
- Place the sliced chicken in a resealable plastic bag or shallow dish. Pour half of the marinade over the chicken, making sure each strip is coated. Reserve the other half of the marinade for later. Marinate the chicken in the refrigerator for at least 30 minutes.

Cook the Chicken:

- Heat a large skillet over medium-high heat. Add olive oil to the skillet. Cook the marinated chicken strips until they are fully cooked and slightly browned, about 6-8 minutes. Remove the chicken from the skillet and set aside.

Sauté Vegetables:
- In the same skillet, add a bit more olive oil if needed. Sauté the sliced bell peppers and onions until they are tender-crisp, about 5-7 minutes.

Combine Chicken and Vegetables:
- Return the cooked chicken to the skillet with the sautéed vegetables. Pour the reserved marinade over the mixture. Stir well to combine and heat through.

Warm Tortillas:
- Heat the tortillas in the skillet or oven according to package instructions.

Assemble Fajitas:
- Spoon the chicken and vegetable mixture onto the warm tortillas.

Add Toppings:
- Add your favorite toppings such as Greek yogurt, salsa, guacamole, shredded cheese, and fresh cilantro.

Serve:
- Serve these delicious Greek Yogurt Chicken Fajitas immediately and enjoy!

These Greek Yogurt Chicken Fajitas are a flavorful and creamy twist on the classic dish. The yogurt-based marinade adds a tangy and luscious touch to the chicken, creating a delicious meal that's perfect for assembling and customizing with your favorite toppings.

Greek Yogurt Avocado Toast

Ingredients:

- 2 slices whole-grain bread (or bread of your choice)
- 1 ripe avocado
- 1/2 cup Greek yogurt (full-fat or low-fat)
- 1 tablespoon lemon juice
- Salt and black pepper to taste
- Optional toppings: cherry tomatoes, radish slices, red pepper flakes, chia seeds, fresh herbs

Instructions:

Toast the Bread:
- Toast the slices of bread to your liking.

Prepare the Avocado Spread:
- In a bowl, mash the ripe avocado with a fork until smooth. Add Greek yogurt, lemon juice, salt, and black pepper. Mix well to combine.

Spread the Mixture:
- Spread the Greek Yogurt and Avocado mixture evenly onto the toasted bread slices.

Add Toppings:
- Add your favorite toppings, such as halved cherry tomatoes, radish slices, red pepper flakes, chia seeds, or fresh herbs.

Season:
- Sprinkle a bit more salt and black pepper over the top for extra flavor.

Serve:
- Serve the Greek Yogurt Avocado Toast immediately and enjoy!

This Greek Yogurt Avocado Toast is a nutritious and satisfying breakfast or snack option. The creamy combination of Greek yogurt and mashed avocado provides a rich texture, while the toppings add a burst of freshness and flavor. Customize it with your preferred toppings for a delicious and wholesome treat.

Greek Yogurt and Herb Zucchini Noodles

Ingredients:

- 4 medium zucchinis, spiralized into noodles
- 1 cup Greek yogurt (full-fat or low-fat)
- 2 tablespoons fresh dill, chopped
- 2 tablespoons fresh mint, chopped
- 1 tablespoon fresh parsley, chopped
- 2 tablespoons olive oil
- 1 clove garlic, minced
- Zest and juice of 1 lemon
- Salt and black pepper to taste
- Optional garnish: crumbled feta cheese, cherry tomatoes, pine nuts

Instructions:

Prepare Zucchini Noodles:
- Spiralize the zucchinis into noodles using a spiralizer.

Make the Greek Yogurt Herb Dressing:
- In a bowl, combine Greek yogurt, chopped dill, chopped mint, chopped parsley, olive oil, minced garlic, lemon zest, and lemon juice. Mix well.

Toss Zucchini Noodles:
- In a large mixing bowl, toss the zucchini noodles with the Greek yogurt herb dressing until well coated.

Season:
- Season the zucchini noodles with salt and black pepper to taste. Adjust the seasoning as needed.

Optional Garnish:
- Garnish with crumbled feta cheese, halved cherry tomatoes, and pine nuts if desired.

Serve:
- Serve the Greek Yogurt and Herb Zucchini Noodles immediately as a refreshing and light side dish.

Enjoy:
- Enjoy this healthy and flavorful dish that showcases the freshness of zucchini paired with a creamy Greek yogurt and herb dressing.

This Greek Yogurt and Herb Zucchini Noodles recipe is a delightful way to enjoy a light and nutritious dish. The zucchini noodles are tossed in a creamy and herby Greek yogurt dressing, creating a refreshing side that pairs well with various main courses or can be enjoyed on its own.

Greek Yogurt Tiramisu

Ingredients:

For the Greek Yogurt Filling:

- 2 cups Greek yogurt (full-fat or low-fat)
- 1/2 cup powdered sugar
- 1 teaspoon vanilla extract

For the Coffee Soaking Mixture:

- 1 cup strong brewed coffee, cooled to room temperature
- 2 tablespoons coffee liqueur (optional)
- 1 tablespoon sugar (optional)

For Layering:

- Ladyfinger cookies (enough to create two layers)
- Cocoa powder for dusting

Instructions:

Prepare the Greek Yogurt Filling:
- In a bowl, combine Greek yogurt, powdered sugar, and vanilla extract. Mix until smooth and well combined. Set aside.

Prepare the Coffee Soaking Mixture:
- In a shallow dish, mix the brewed coffee with coffee liqueur and sugar (if using). Stir until the sugar is dissolved. Set aside.

Dip Ladyfingers:
- Quickly dip each ladyfinger into the coffee mixture, making sure not to soak them too long to avoid sogginess.

Layer the Tiramisu:
- In a serving dish, create a layer of dipped ladyfingers at the bottom.

Add Greek Yogurt Filling:
- Spread half of the Greek yogurt filling over the layer of ladyfingers.

Repeat the Layers:
- Repeat the process with another layer of dipped ladyfingers and the remaining Greek yogurt filling.

Chill:

- Cover the tiramisu and refrigerate for at least 4 hours or overnight to allow the flavors to meld and the dessert to set.

Dust with Cocoa Powder:
- Before serving, dust the top of the tiramisu with cocoa powder using a fine sieve.

Slice and Serve:
- Slice and serve this delightful Greek Yogurt Tiramisu chilled.

Enjoy:
- Enjoy this lighter version of tiramisu with the creamy goodness of Greek yogurt.

This Greek Yogurt Tiramisu offers a healthier twist on the classic Italian dessert. The combination of rich Greek yogurt, coffee-soaked ladyfingers, and a dusting of cocoa powder creates a delightful treat that's perfect for indulging without the guilt.

Greek Yogurt and Honey Glazed Carrots

Ingredients:

- 1 pound baby carrots, washed and trimmed
- 1/2 cup Greek yogurt (full-fat or low-fat)
- 2 tablespoons honey
- 1 tablespoon olive oil
- 1 teaspoon Dijon mustard
- 1 teaspoon fresh thyme leaves
- Salt and black pepper to taste
- Chopped fresh parsley for garnish (optional)

Instructions:

Steam the Carrots:
- Place the baby carrots in a steamer basket and steam until they are tender but still have a slight crunch, about 5-7 minutes. Alternatively, you can boil the carrots in water until they are just tender.

Prepare the Greek Yogurt Glaze:
- In a bowl, whisk together Greek yogurt, honey, olive oil, Dijon mustard, fresh thyme leaves, salt, and black pepper. Mix until well combined.

Coat the Carrots:
- Once the carrots are cooked, transfer them to a bowl. Pour the Greek yogurt glaze over the carrots and gently toss until they are well coated.

Serve:
- Transfer the glazed carrots to a serving dish.

Garnish (Optional):
- Garnish with chopped fresh parsley if desired.

Enjoy:
- Serve these Greek Yogurt and Honey Glazed Carrots as a delicious and healthy side dish.

This recipe combines the natural sweetness of honey with the creamy texture of Greek yogurt to create a flavorful glaze for tender baby carrots. The addition of thyme adds a savory touch, making these glazed carrots a perfect side dish for a variety of meals.

Greek Yogurt Chicken Caesar Wrap

Ingredients:

For the Greek Yogurt Caesar Dressing:

- 1 cup Greek yogurt (full-fat or low-fat)
- 2 tablespoons grated Parmesan cheese
- 1 tablespoon Dijon mustard
- 2 cloves garlic, minced
- 2 anchovy fillets, minced (optional)
- 1 tablespoon fresh lemon juice
- 1 teaspoon Worcestershire sauce
- Salt and black pepper to taste

For the Chicken Filling:

- 2 cups cooked and shredded chicken breast
- 1 cup cherry tomatoes, halved
- 1 cup cucumber, diced
- 1/4 cup red onion, finely chopped
- 1/4 cup black olives, sliced
- 4 large whole-grain or spinach tortillas
- Romaine lettuce leaves

Instructions:

Prepare the Greek Yogurt Caesar Dressing:
- In a bowl, whisk together Greek yogurt, grated Parmesan cheese, Dijon mustard, minced garlic, minced anchovies (if using), lemon juice, Worcestershire sauce, salt, and black pepper. Adjust the seasoning to taste. Set aside.

Combine Chicken Filling:
- In a separate bowl, combine shredded chicken, cherry tomatoes, diced cucumber, chopped red onion, and sliced black olives.

Mix with Dressing:

- Add a generous amount of the Greek Yogurt Caesar dressing to the chicken mixture. Toss until well coated.

Assemble the Wraps:
- Lay out the tortillas. Place a few Romaine lettuce leaves on each tortilla.

Add Chicken Filling:
- Spoon the Greek Yogurt Caesar chicken filling over the lettuce.

Wrap:
- Fold in the sides of the tortilla and then roll it up tightly, creating a wrap.

Serve:
- Serve the Greek Yogurt Chicken Caesar Wraps immediately.

Enjoy:
- Enjoy these delicious and wholesome wraps as a satisfying lunch or dinner option.

These Greek Yogurt Chicken Caesar Wraps offer a healthier twist on the classic Caesar wrap by using a creamy Greek yogurt dressing. Packed with protein and crisp veggies, they make for a satisfying and flavorful meal.

Greek Yogurt and Pumpkin Bread

Ingredients:

- 1 3/4 cups all-purpose flour
- 1 teaspoon baking soda
- 1/2 teaspoon baking powder
- 1/2 teaspoon salt
- 1 teaspoon ground cinnamon
- 1/2 teaspoon ground nutmeg
- 1/2 teaspoon ground ginger
- 1/4 teaspoon ground cloves
- 1 cup canned pumpkin puree
- 1/2 cup Greek yogurt (full-fat or low-fat)
- 1/2 cup unsalted butter, softened
- 1 cup granulated sugar
- 1/2 cup brown sugar, packed
- 2 large eggs
- 1 teaspoon vanilla extract

Instructions:

Preheat the Oven:
- Preheat your oven to 350°F (175°C). Grease and flour a 9x5-inch loaf pan.

Whisk Dry Ingredients:
- In a medium bowl, whisk together the flour, baking soda, baking powder, salt, cinnamon, nutmeg, ginger, and cloves. Set aside.

Mix Pumpkin and Greek Yogurt:
- In another bowl, combine the pumpkin puree and Greek yogurt. Mix well and set aside.

Cream Butter and Sugars:
- In a large mixing bowl, cream together the softened butter, granulated sugar, and brown sugar until light and fluffy.

Add Eggs and Vanilla:
- Add the eggs one at a time, beating well after each addition. Stir in the vanilla extract.

Combine Wet and Dry Ingredients:
- Gradually add the dry ingredients to the wet ingredients, mixing until just combined.

Alternate with Pumpkin Mixture:
- Alternate adding the dry ingredients and the pumpkin mixture to the batter, beginning and ending with the dry ingredients. Mix until just combined.

Bake:
- Pour the batter into the prepared loaf pan. Smooth the top with a spatula. Bake in the preheated oven for 60-70 minutes or until a toothpick inserted into the center comes out clean.

Cool:
- Allow the pumpkin bread to cool in the pan for about 10 minutes, then transfer it to a wire rack to cool completely.

Slice and Serve:
- Once cooled, slice and serve the Greek Yogurt and Pumpkin Bread.

Enjoy:
- Enjoy this moist and flavorful pumpkin bread with the added creaminess of Greek yogurt.

This Greek Yogurt and Pumpkin Bread combines the warm flavors of fall with the richness of Greek yogurt for a delicious and moist treat. It's perfect for enjoying with a cup of coffee or tea on a cozy autumn day.

Greek Yogurt and Berry Cobbler

Ingredients:

For the Berry Filling:

- 4 cups mixed berries (strawberries, blueberries, raspberries, blackberries)
- 1/2 cup granulated sugar
- 2 tablespoons cornstarch
- 1 tablespoon lemon juice

For the Greek Yogurt Biscuit Topping:

- 1 cup all-purpose flour
- 1/4 cup granulated sugar
- 1 teaspoon baking powder
- 1/4 teaspoon baking soda
- 1/4 teaspoon salt
- 1/2 cup unsalted butter, cold and cut into small pieces
- 1 cup Greek yogurt (full-fat or low-fat)
- 1 teaspoon vanilla extract

For Topping:

- 1 tablespoon granulated sugar (for sprinkling)

Instructions:

Preheat the Oven:
- Preheat your oven to 375°F (190°C). Grease a baking dish or casserole.

Prepare the Berry Filling:
- In a bowl, combine the mixed berries, granulated sugar, cornstarch, and lemon juice. Toss until the berries are coated evenly. Transfer the berry mixture to the prepared baking dish.

Make the Greek Yogurt Biscuit Topping:
- In a large bowl, whisk together the flour, sugar, baking powder, baking soda, and salt. Add the cold butter pieces and use a pastry cutter or your fingers to incorporate the butter into the dry ingredients until the mixture resembles coarse crumbs.

Add Greek Yogurt and Vanilla:

- Stir in the Greek yogurt and vanilla extract until just combined. Do not overmix; the dough should be slightly lumpy.

Drop Biscuit Dough:
- Drop spoonfuls of the biscuit dough evenly over the berry filling, covering it as much as possible.

Sprinkle with Sugar:
- Sprinkle the top of the biscuit dough with 1 tablespoon of granulated sugar for a golden finish.

Bake:
- Bake in the preheated oven for 30-35 minutes or until the topping is golden brown, and the berry filling is bubbly.

Cool:
- Allow the cobbler to cool for a few minutes before serving.

Serve:
- Serve the Greek Yogurt and Berry Cobbler warm. It pairs well with a scoop of vanilla ice cream or a dollop of Greek yogurt.

Enjoy:
- Enjoy this delightful Greek Yogurt and Berry Cobbler as a comforting and fruity dessert.

This Greek Yogurt and Berry Cobbler brings together the sweetness of mixed berries with a tender Greek yogurt biscuit topping. It's a perfect dessert to showcase seasonal berries, and the addition of Greek yogurt adds a creamy and tangy element to the cobbler.

Greek Yogurt and Herb Stuffed Chicken Breast

Ingredients:

For the Greek Yogurt and Herb Filling:

- 1 cup Greek yogurt (full-fat or low-fat)
- 1/4 cup feta cheese, crumbled
- 2 tablespoons fresh dill, chopped
- 2 tablespoons fresh parsley, chopped
- 1 tablespoon fresh mint, chopped
- 2 cloves garlic, minced
- Salt and black pepper to taste

For the Chicken:

- 4 boneless, skinless chicken breasts
- 2 tablespoons olive oil
- 1 teaspoon dried oregano
- 1 teaspoon smoked paprika
- Salt and black pepper to taste

Instructions:

Preheat the Oven:
- Preheat your oven to 375°F (190°C).

Prepare the Greek Yogurt and Herb Filling:
- In a bowl, combine Greek yogurt, crumbled feta cheese, chopped dill, chopped parsley, chopped mint, minced garlic, salt, and black pepper. Mix well to create the herb filling.

Butterfly the Chicken Breasts:
- Lay the chicken breasts on a cutting board. Carefully cut horizontally into the thickest part of each breast, creating a pocket without cutting all the way through.

Stuff the Chicken:
- Stuff each chicken breast with the Greek Yogurt and Herb filling, dividing it evenly among the breasts.

Secure with Toothpicks:
- Secure the openings with toothpicks to keep the filling inside during cooking.

Season the Chicken:
- In a small bowl, mix olive oil, dried oregano, smoked paprika, salt, and black pepper. Brush the seasoned oil over the stuffed chicken breasts.

Sear the Chicken:
- Heat an oven-safe skillet over medium-high heat. Sear the stuffed chicken breasts on each side until browned, about 2-3 minutes per side.

Transfer to Oven:
- Transfer the skillet to the preheated oven and bake for 20-25 minutes or until the chicken is cooked through and reaches an internal temperature of 165°F (74°C).

Rest and Serve:
- Allow the stuffed chicken breasts to rest for a few minutes before removing the toothpicks. Slice and serve.

Enjoy:
- Enjoy this Greek Yogurt and Herb Stuffed Chicken Breast with a side of vegetables or a light salad.

This dish combines the creamy goodness of Greek yogurt with a mix of fresh herbs and feta cheese, creating a flavorful stuffing for tender chicken breasts. It's a delicious and elegant option for a wholesome meal.

Greek Yogurt and Chia Seed Pudding

Ingredients:

- 1 cup Greek yogurt (full-fat or low-fat)
- 1/4 cup chia seeds
- 1-2 tablespoons honey or maple syrup (adjust to taste)
- 1 teaspoon vanilla extract
- 1 cup milk (dairy or plant-based)
- Fresh berries, sliced fruits, or nuts for topping

Instructions:

Mix Greek Yogurt and Chia Seeds:
- In a bowl, combine Greek yogurt, chia seeds, honey or maple syrup, and vanilla extract. Mix well to ensure the chia seeds are evenly distributed.

Add Milk:
- Pour in the milk and stir until all the ingredients are well combined.

Refrigerate:
- Cover the bowl and refrigerate the mixture for at least 4 hours or overnight. This allows the chia seeds to absorb the liquid and create a pudding-like consistency.

Stir and Adjust Consistency:
- After the initial refrigeration, give the mixture a good stir. If the pudding is too thick, you can add a bit more milk to reach your desired consistency.

Serve:
- Spoon the Greek Yogurt and Chia Seed Pudding into serving bowls or glasses.

Top with Fresh Fruits or Nuts:
- Top the pudding with fresh berries, sliced fruits, or nuts for added texture and flavor.

Enjoy:
- Enjoy this nutritious and satisfying Greek Yogurt and Chia Seed Pudding as a breakfast, snack, or dessert option.

This recipe combines the creamy texture of Greek yogurt with the nutritional powerhouse of chia seeds to create a delightful pudding. It's not only delicious but also packed with protein, fiber, and healthy fats. Customize it with your favorite toppings for a tasty and wholesome treat.